Contents

Christmas themed worksheets 1

Colour by number pictures using colours in French 9

Christmas presents 14

Winter / Father Christmas' clothes 18

Christmas word searches 24

Christmas games (board game style) 28

Christmas cards to colour 34

Happy new year card to colour 45

French - English word list 47

Answers 48

Lets meet Père Noël !

In the conversation below, **Père Noël** (Father Christmas) says hello and asks the boy what he is called. The boy replies in French with Hello! My name is Paul.

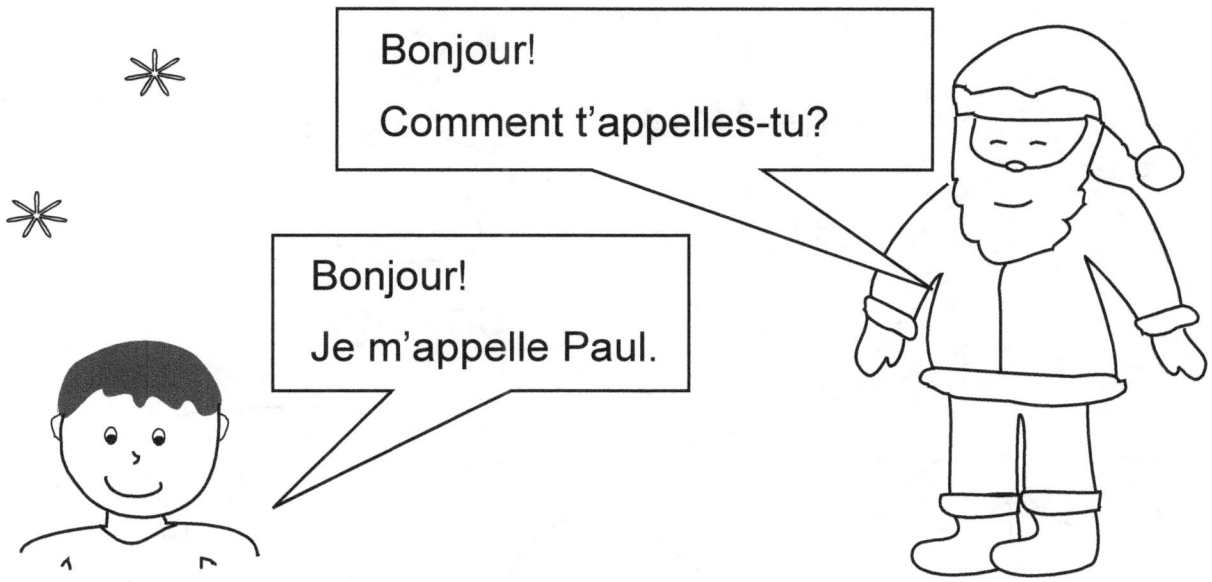

> Bonjour!
> Comment t'appelles-tu?

> Bonjour!
> Je m'appelle Paul.

1) Imagine you met Père Noël in France! Copy "**Bonjour! Je m'appelle**" then write your own name:

Bonjour!   Je   m'appelle ✏️

_____   __   _____   _____ .

2) If Père Noël asked you "**Comment ça va?**" (How are you?), what would you reply? Circle one phrase that you would say from the phrases below:

Ça va bien.   Comme ci comme ça.   Ça va mal
(I am good)   (I am okay / so-so)   (I am not so good)

3) Now a very important question for Père Noël. He needs to know where you live! **Où habites-tu?** (Where do you live?) Copy J'habite à (then add a city or a town).

J'habite   à

_____   __ _____ .

> A lot of towns & cities keep the same name in French. Here though are two cities which change:
> Londre = London
> Edimbourg = Edinburgh

Noël (Christmas)

Copier les mots et les dessins: (Copy the words and the pictures:)

Père Noël
Père Noël

un sapin

un cadeau

un renne

un ange

une étoile

Un pull de Noël (A Christmas jumper)

Design a Christmas jumper with the following on it:

trois sapins   cinq étoiles    deux bonhommes de neige   huit cadeaux

1	2	3	4	5	6	7	8
un	deux	trois	quatre	cinq	six	sept	huit

Combien y en a-t-il ? (How many are there?)

| 1 = un | 2 = deux | 3 = trois | 4 = quatre | 5 = cinq |

deux

_____ sapins   _____ cadeaux

_____ cartes   _____ rennes

_____ bonhommes de neige

Les cadeaux (presents)

Dessiner la quantité correcte de cadeaux:
(Draw the correct number of presents:)

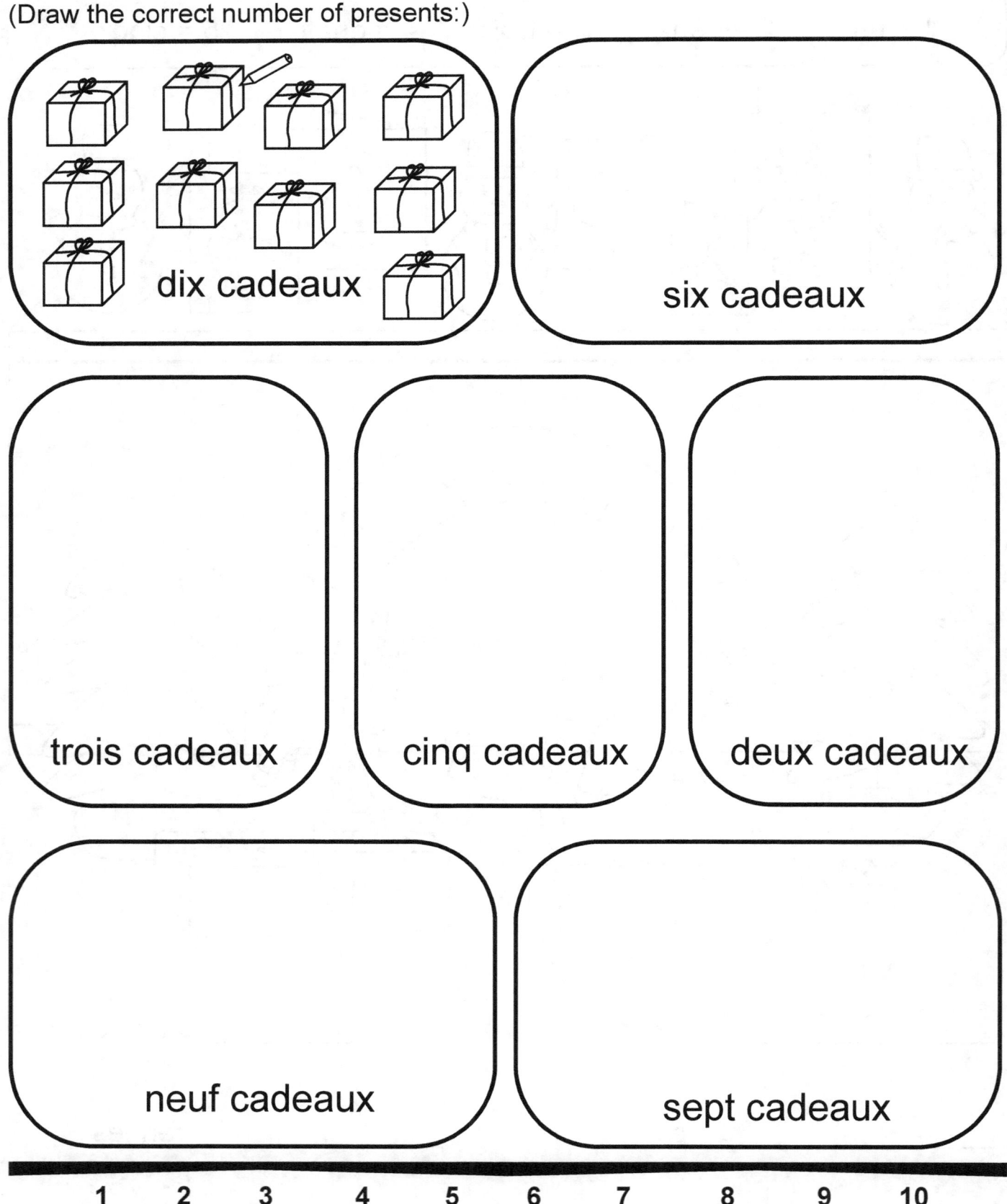

1	2	3	4	5	6	7	8	9	10
un	deux	trois	quatre	cinq	six	sept	huit	neuf	dix

Les couleurs

rouge = red   bleu = blue   jaune = yellow   orange = orange   vert = green
gris = grey   blanc = white   violet = lilac   marron = brown   noir = black

Les cadeaux (presents)

Compter et colorier les cadeaux: (Count and colour the presents:)

 cinq en jaune (5 in yellow)  deux en bleu (2 in blue)   trois en rouge (3 in red)

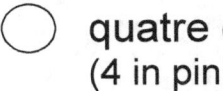 quatre en rose (4 in pink) △ six en vert (six in green)

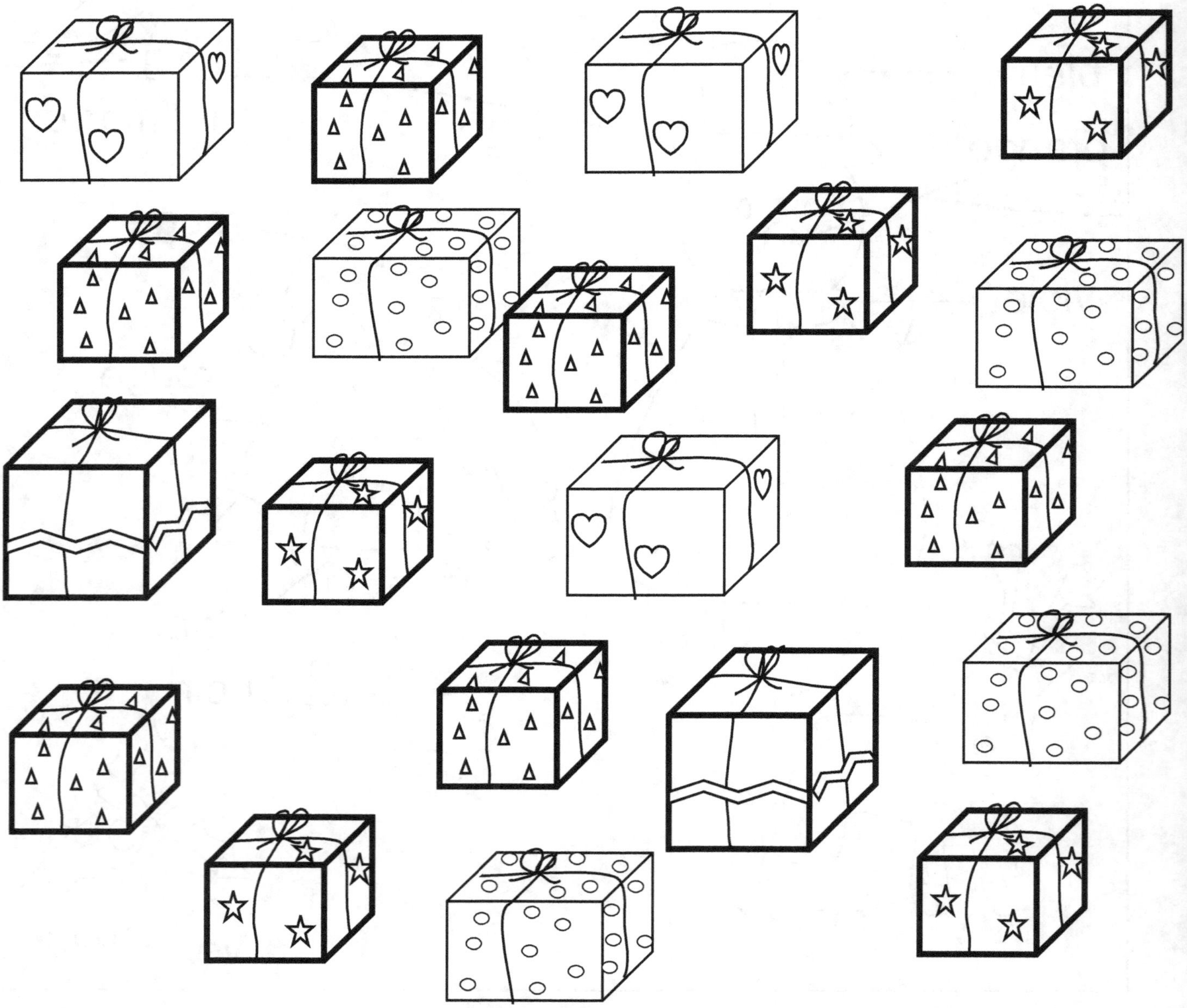

rouge = red   bleu = blue   jaune = yellow   vert = green   rose = pink

Colorier la chaussette de Noël !

(Colour the Christmas sock)

1 = jaune
2 = violet
3 = vert
4 = rose
5 = gris
6 = rouge
7 = marron
8 = noir
9 = orange
10 = bleu
11 = blanc

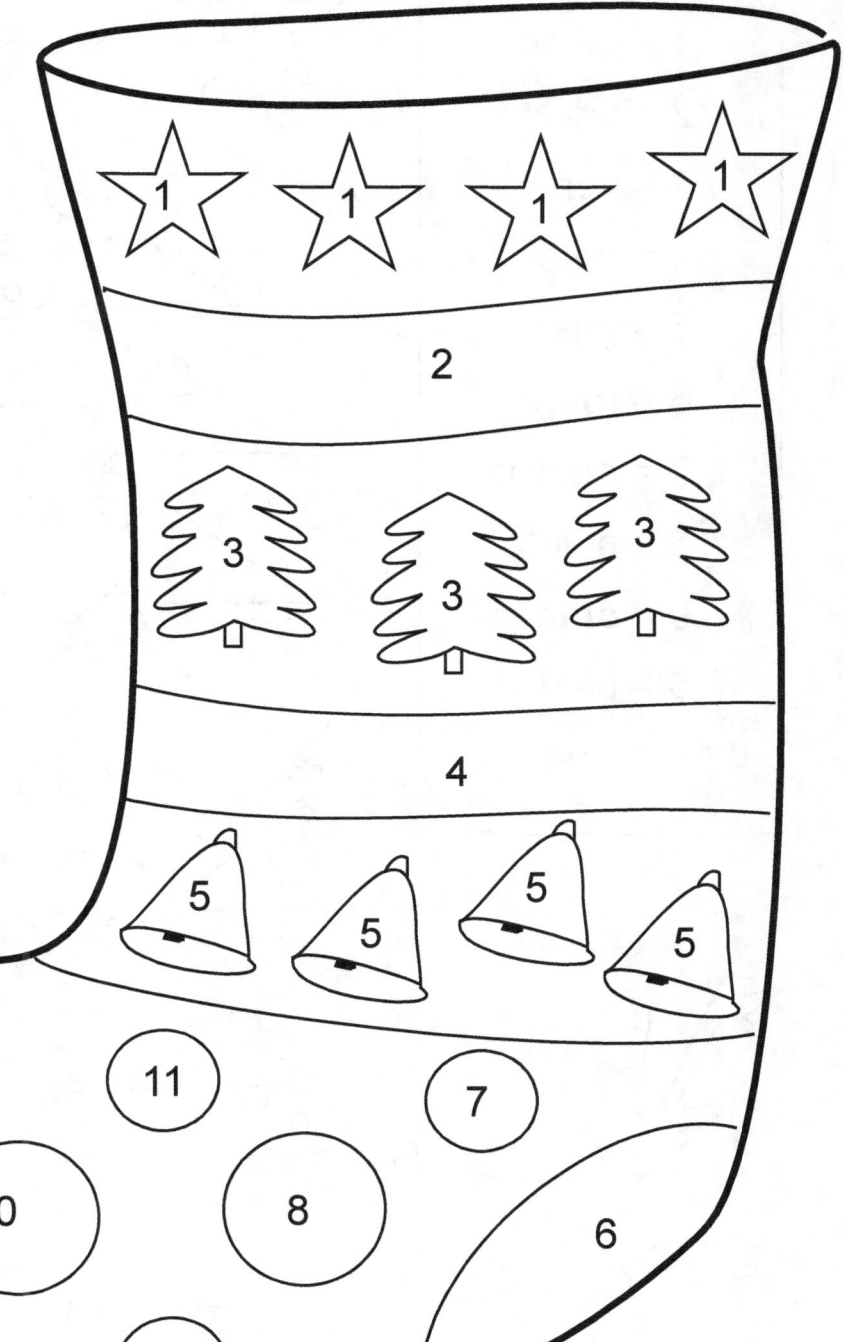

 rouge = red bleu = blue jaune = yellow vert = green
noir = black gris = grey violet = lilac rose = pink
marron = brown orange = orange blanc = white

Colorier le dessin !
(Colour the picture!)

1 = jaune
2 = violet
3 = vert
4 = rose
5 = gris
6 = rouge
7 = marron
8 = noir
9 = orange
10 = bleu
11 = blanc

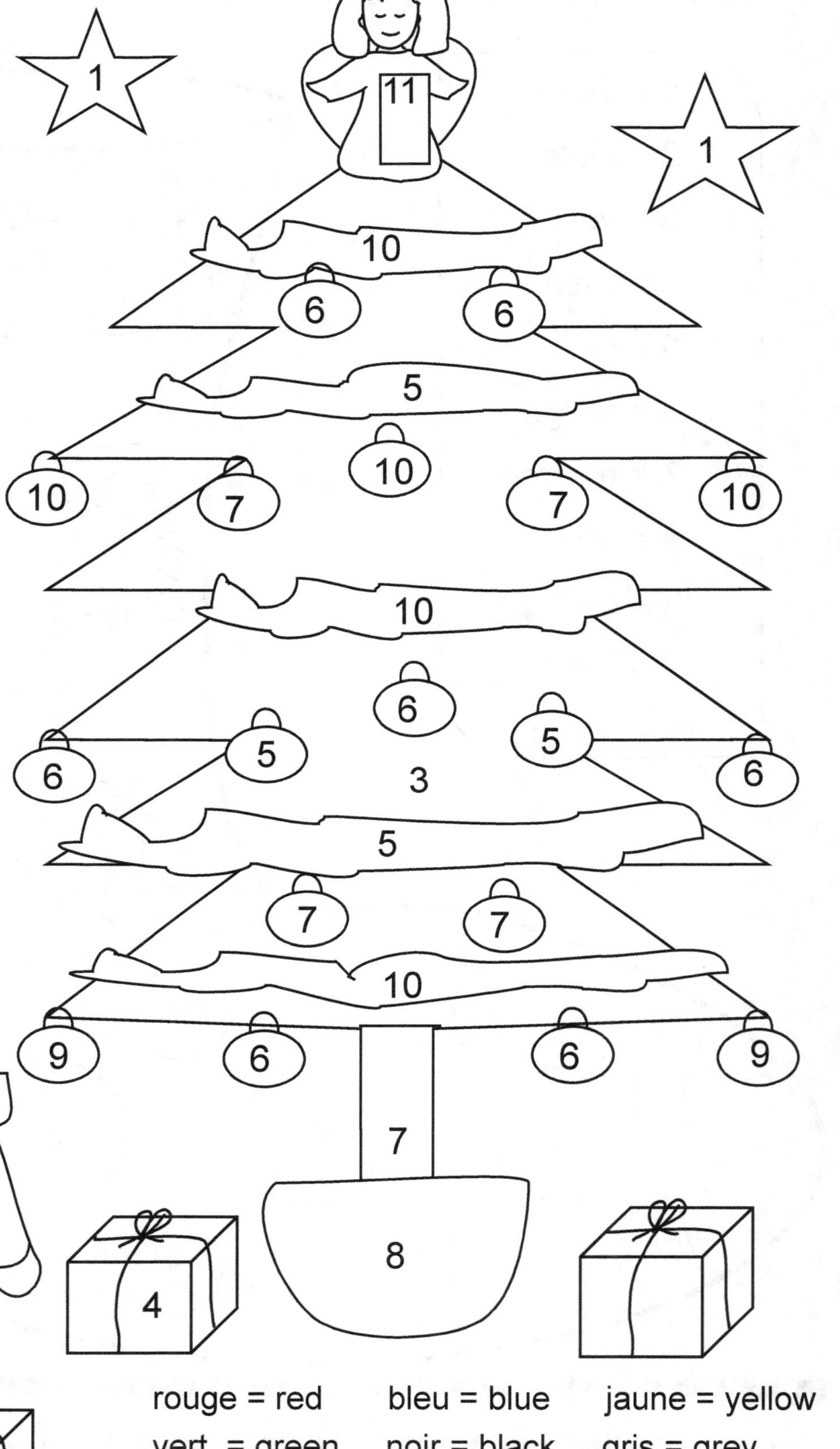

rouge = red
vert = green
violet = lilac
marron = brown

bleu = blue
noir = black
rose = pink
orange = orange

jaune = yellow
gris = grey
blanc = white

Colorier les décorations

(Colour the decorations)

1 =	jaune
2 =	violet
3 =	vert
4 =	rose
5 =	gris
6 =	rouge
7 =	marron
8 =	noir
9 =	orange
10 =	bleu
11 =	blanc

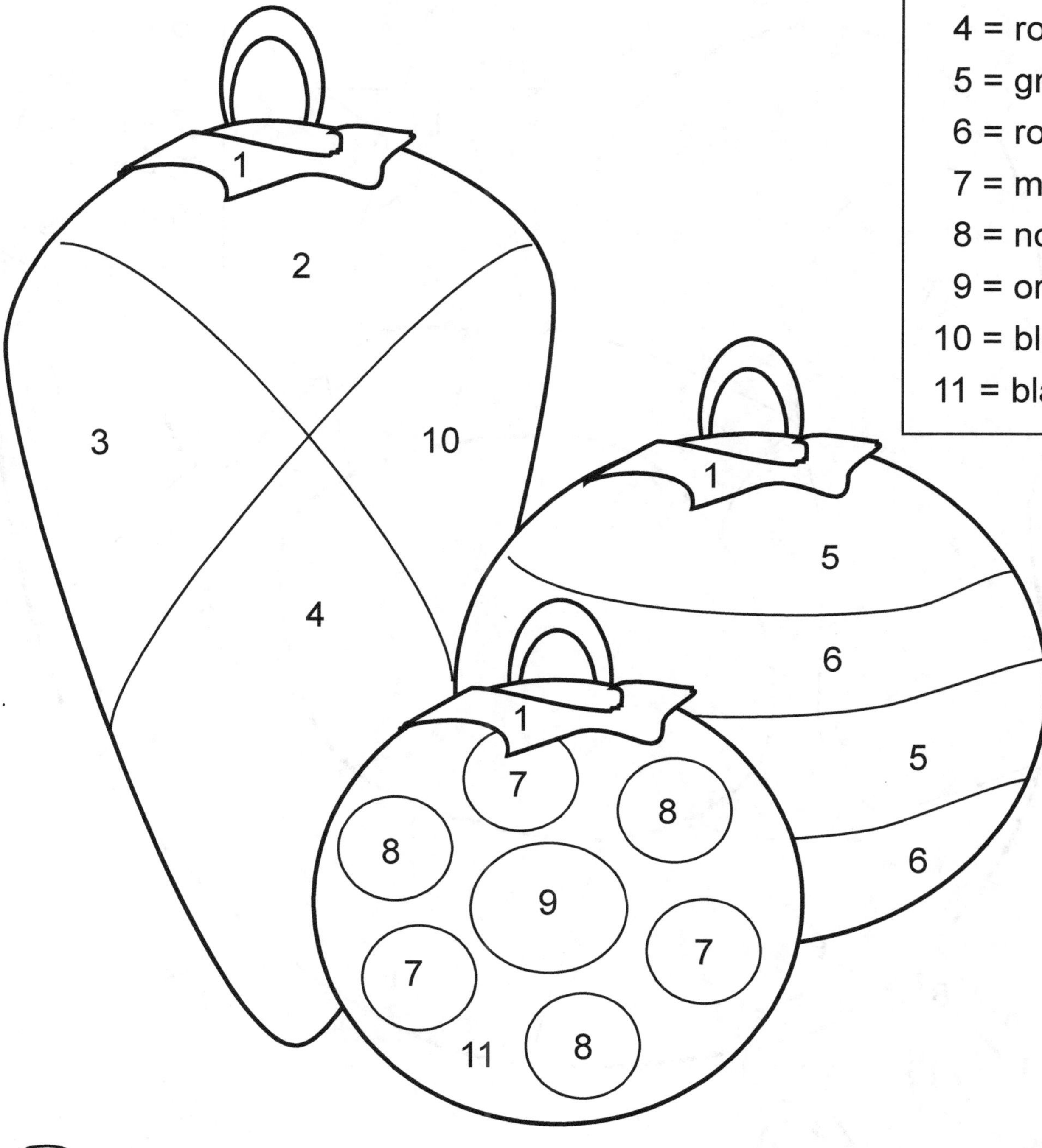

rouge = red bleu = blue jaune = yellow vert = green
noir = black gris = grey violet = lilac rose = pink
blanc = white marron = brown orange = orange

Le rouge-gorge (the robin)

Colorier le rouge-gorge: (Colour the robin)

1 = jaune
2 = violet
3 = vert
4 = rose
5 = gris
6 = rouge
7 = marron
8 = noir
9 = orange

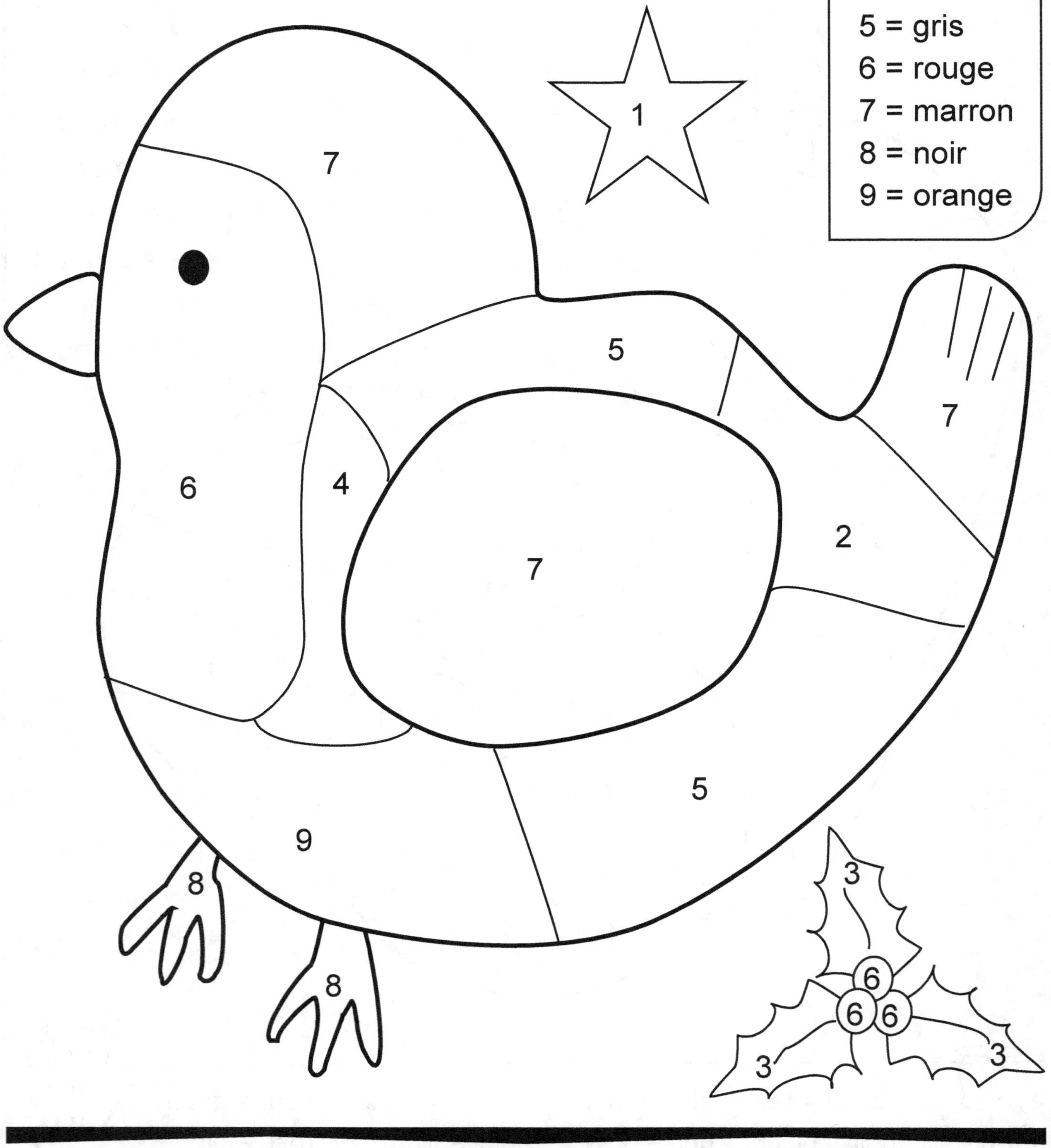

rouge = red   jaune = yellow   vert = green   noir = black   gris = grey
violet = lilac rose = pink   marron = brown   orange = orange

Colorier les cloches et les étoiles!
(Colour the bells and the stars!)

1 = jaune
2 = violet
3 = vert
4 = rose
5 = gris
6 = rouge
7 = marron
8 = noir
9 = orange
10 = bleu
11 = blanc

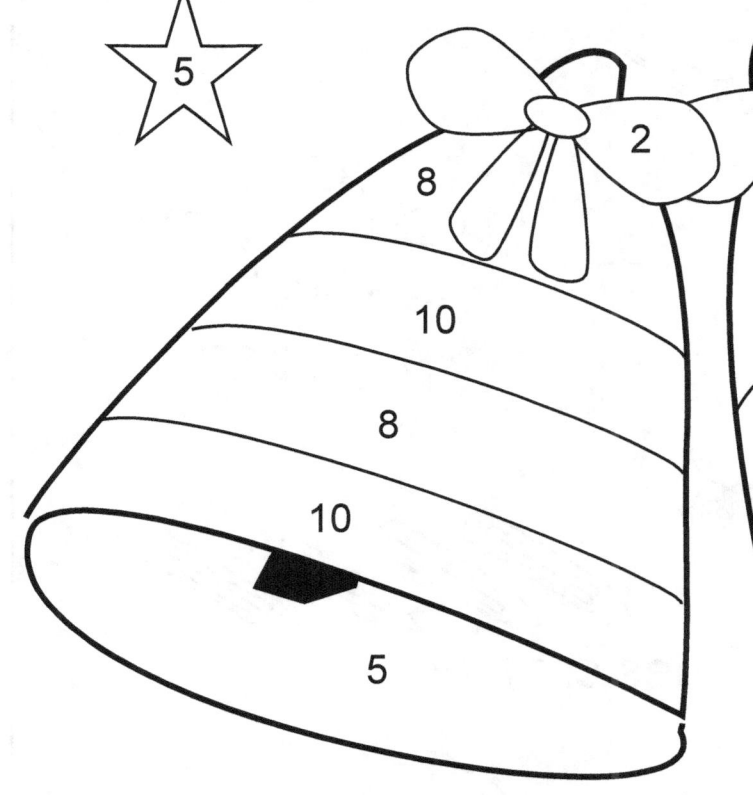
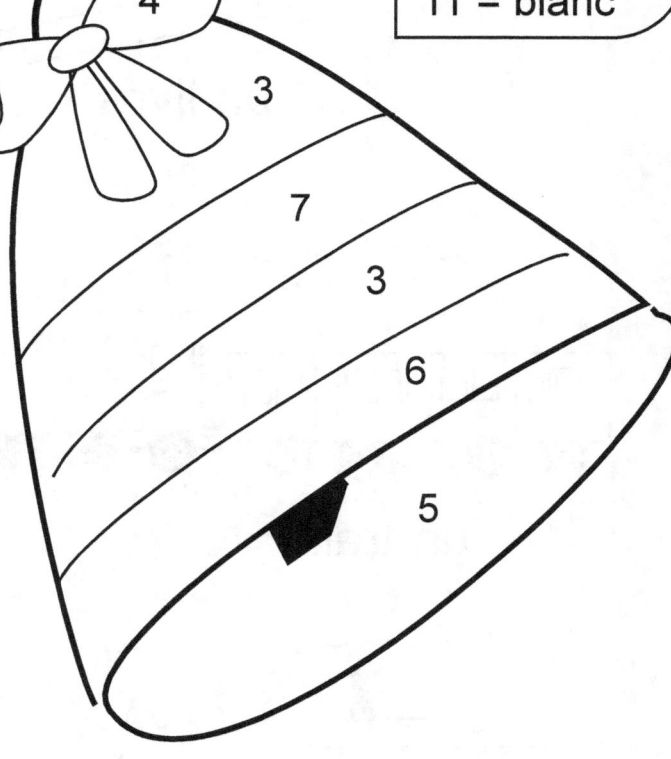

rouge = red   bleu = blue   jaune = yellow
vert = green   noir = black   gris = grey
violet = lilac rose = pink   blanc = white
marron = brown orange = orange

Les cadeaux (the presents)

une poupée

un ballon

un nounours

un livre

des bonbons

un train

des crayons

un bateau

une voiture

Les cadeaux (the presents)

Écrire les mots en français:
(Write the words in French:)

une voiture 🖉

1) _____

2) _____

3) _____

4) _____

5) _____

6) _____

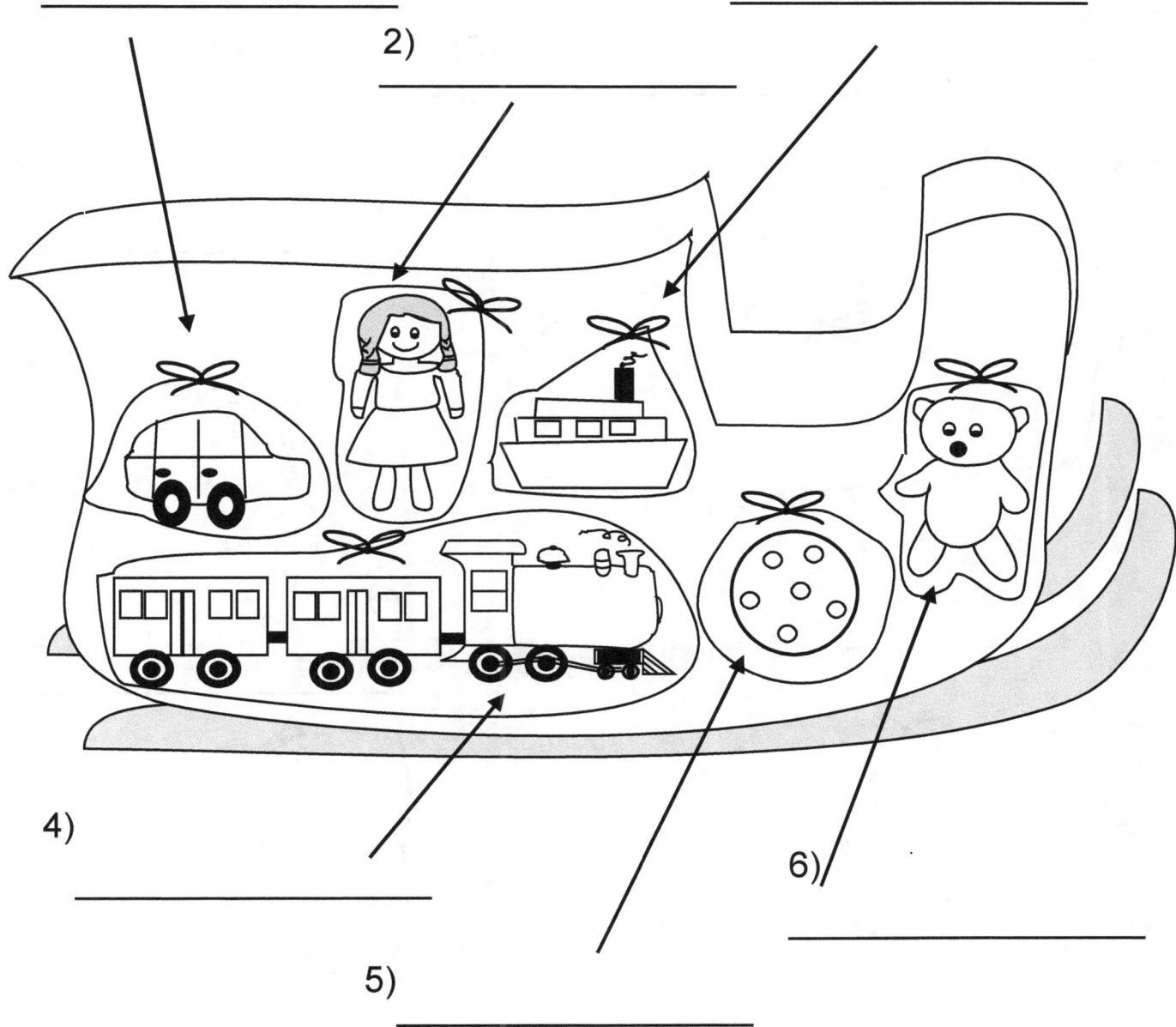

une voiture = a car   un train = a train   un bateau = a boat

une poupée = a doll   un ballon = a ball   un nounours = a teddy

Qu'est-ce que c'est? (What is it?)

Père Noël has forgotten what presents he's wrapped up!

Look at the toys in the sleigh on the previous page.
Write the French word for each toy:

1)  *un nounours*

2)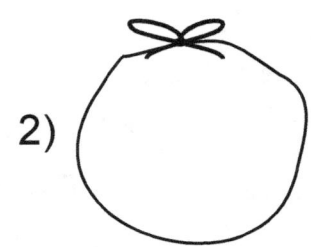
_____

3)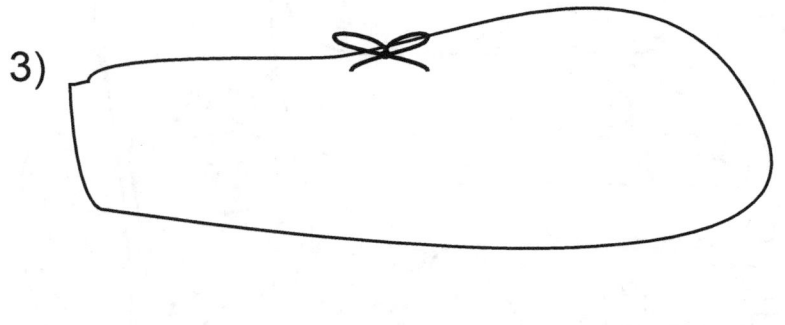

4)
_____

_____

5)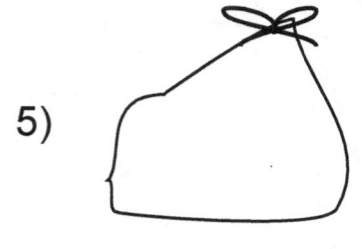

6)

_____

_____

 une voiture    un train    un bateau    une poupée    un ballon    un nounours

Qu'est-ce que tu veux pour Noël?
(What do you want for Christmas?)

Je voudrais _____   **I would like _____**

des bonbons   des crayons   un bateau   un nounours   un ballon   une voiture   un train

1) Lire les phrases et faire un dessin:
(Read the sentences and do a drawing:)

a) Je voudrais une voiture.

b) Je voudrais des crayons.

c) Je voudrais des bonbons.

d) Je voudrais un nounours.

2) Écrire ce que tu veux pour Noël:
(Write what you would like for Christmas:)

Pour Noël, je voudrais:

Les vêtements (clothes)

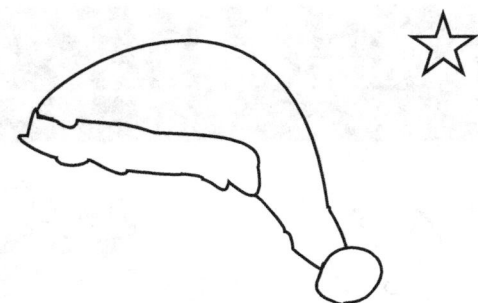
un bonnet de Noël

un manteau

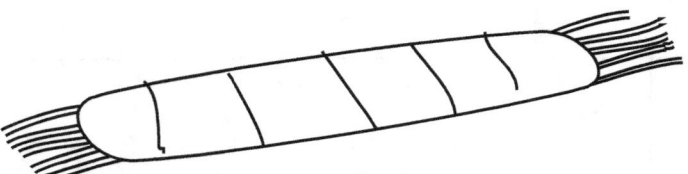
une écharpe

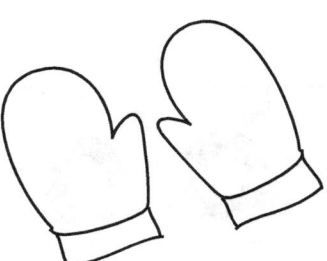
des gants

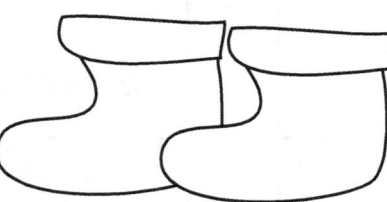
des bottes

un pull

un pantalon

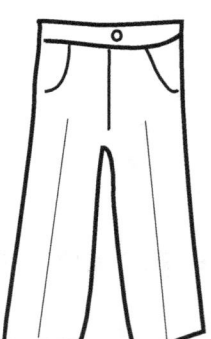
des chaussettes

Copier les mots et les dessins

(Copy the words and the pictures:)

Qu'est-ce que c'est? (What is it?)

Écrire les mots en français: (Write the words in French:)

1)
un bonnet de Noël
_____

2)
_____

3)
_____

4)
_____

5)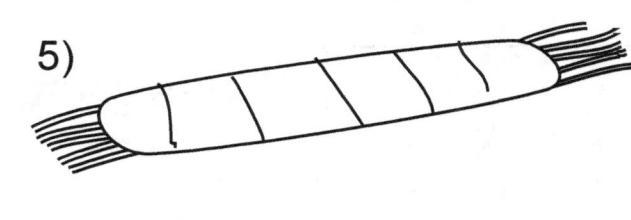
_____

6)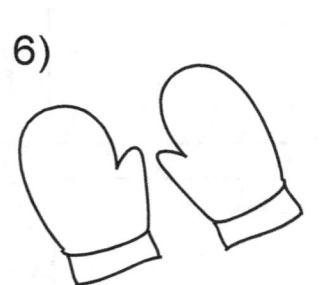
_____

7)
_____

8)
_____

un bonnet de Noël — un manteau — un pull — un pantalon — une écharpe — des gants — des bottes — des chaussettes

Qu'est-ce qu'il porte? (What is he wearing?)

1) Écrire les mots en français: (Write the words in French:)

> des gants marron = brown gloves un pantalon rouge = red trousers
> des bottes noires = black boots
> un bonnet rouge et blanc = a red and white hat
> un manteau rouge et blanc = a red and white coat

a) *un bonnet rouge et blanc*

b) _____

c) _____

d) _____

e) _____

2) Vrai ou faux? (True or false?):

Père Noël porte = Father Chrismas is wearing

a) Père Noël porte un bonnet bleu. _____
b) Père Noël porte un pantalon rouge. _____
c) Père Noël porte un manteau noir. _____
d) Père Noël porte un un manteau rouge et blanc. _____

J'ai beaucoup de cadeaux!

(I've lots of presents!)

mon frère (my brother)   ma soeur (my sister)   mon père (my dad)   ma mère (my mum)   mon grand-père (my grand father)   ma grand-mère (my grand mother)

Écrire en français les mots qui manquent:
(Write in French the missing words:)

Salut!

J'ai beaucoup de cadeaux pour ma famille!
(I've lots of presents for my family!)

un manteau

Pour ma mère, j'ai _____ .
(For my mum, I have)

Pour mon père, j'ai _____ .

Pour ma soeur, j'ai _____ .

Pour mon frère, j'ai _____ .

Pour ma grand-mère, j'ai _____ .

Pour mon grand-père, j'ai _____ .

Salut!

Anne Marie

---

un pull = a jumper   une écharpe = a scarf   des chaussettes = some socks
un manteau = a coat   un bonnet de Noël = Christmas hat   des gants = some gloves

Compter les pulls et colorier:

(Count the jumpers and colour:)

| 2 deux en rouge | 3 trois en marron | 4 quatre en vert | 3 trois en gris | 4 quatre en bleu |

rouge = red   marron = brown   vert = green   gris = grey   bleu = blue

C'est Noël ! (It's Christmas)

Trouver ces mots: (Find these words:)

- BONHOMME DE NEIGE
- PÈRE NOËL
- SAPIN
- ÉTOILE
- CADEAU
- NOËL
- DÉCORATIONS
- RENNE
- ANGE
- CARTE
- CLOCHE

					L						
				Ë	K	L					
			O	T	H	I	O				
		N	E	S	A	P	I	N			
		W	Q	Z	P	E	U	Y			
	J	K	O	P	L	G	F	R	O		
	N	O	Y	I	G	F	B	E	V		
Z	S	E	O	J	K	Y	B	N	L	Z	
N	J	T	L	R	E	N	B	N	G	Z	
Q	Z	É	S	A	N	G	E	L	E	U	G	B
P	E	R	H	G	G	B	O	N	H	O	M	C
R	E	N	X	F	C	A	D	E	A	U	J	K	A	H
X	D	K	L	D	E	C	O	R	Y	H	G	B	R	X
B	O	C	L	O	C	H	E	N	H	J	N	W	H	T	J	K
X	D	E	G	K	L	H	Y	G	H	G	B	U	J	E	L	O
Z	D	É	C	O	R	A	T	I	O	N	S	A	E	G	E	G	E	L
C	A	D	E	Y	H	G	B	G	L	U	G	E	T	O	J	K	H	G
S	J	K	S	A	P	Y	T	G	B	P	È	R	E	N	O	Ë	L	C
F	H	G	G	C	A	D	E	N	G	Y	H	E	T	O	I	G	F	V	K	O
S	A	P	I	G	J	J	G	F	E	J	K	G	F	C	L	O	C	Y	G	H	G
B	O	N	H	O	M	M	E	D	E	N	E	I	G	E	J	K	G	Y	S	X

Les couleurs (colours)

```
              J
            V A J
            X U K
            A N U
          W D E G R
          P L H I G
          Q W O J K
K Y H G F H J O N P H G B R O U G E Q W
  B L A N C J K Y G F B J K L I G F F
    I K H N B H G F V I O L E T V C
      I K H N G E B G F T H J U G
        Q E H S G B J K I K G G
          N O J Y H M A R U R
          R Y O R A N G E H I
          V E R G F T H U B S
        B V M A R R O N U J H Y
      L O J H G Y G V F Q X Z D O
    K I J H J U G     Q G C D E G U
    V E R T K U       J H Y G E O
    N H Y J K         I H L G Y
    E N J Y           B J Y I
    L Y               W D
```

Trouver ces mots: (Find these words:)

VERT    JAUNE   ROUGE   NOIR    VIOLET   ROSE

GRIS   ORANGE    MARRON    BLEU   BLANC

Les vêtements (clothes)

Trouver ces mots: (Find these words:)

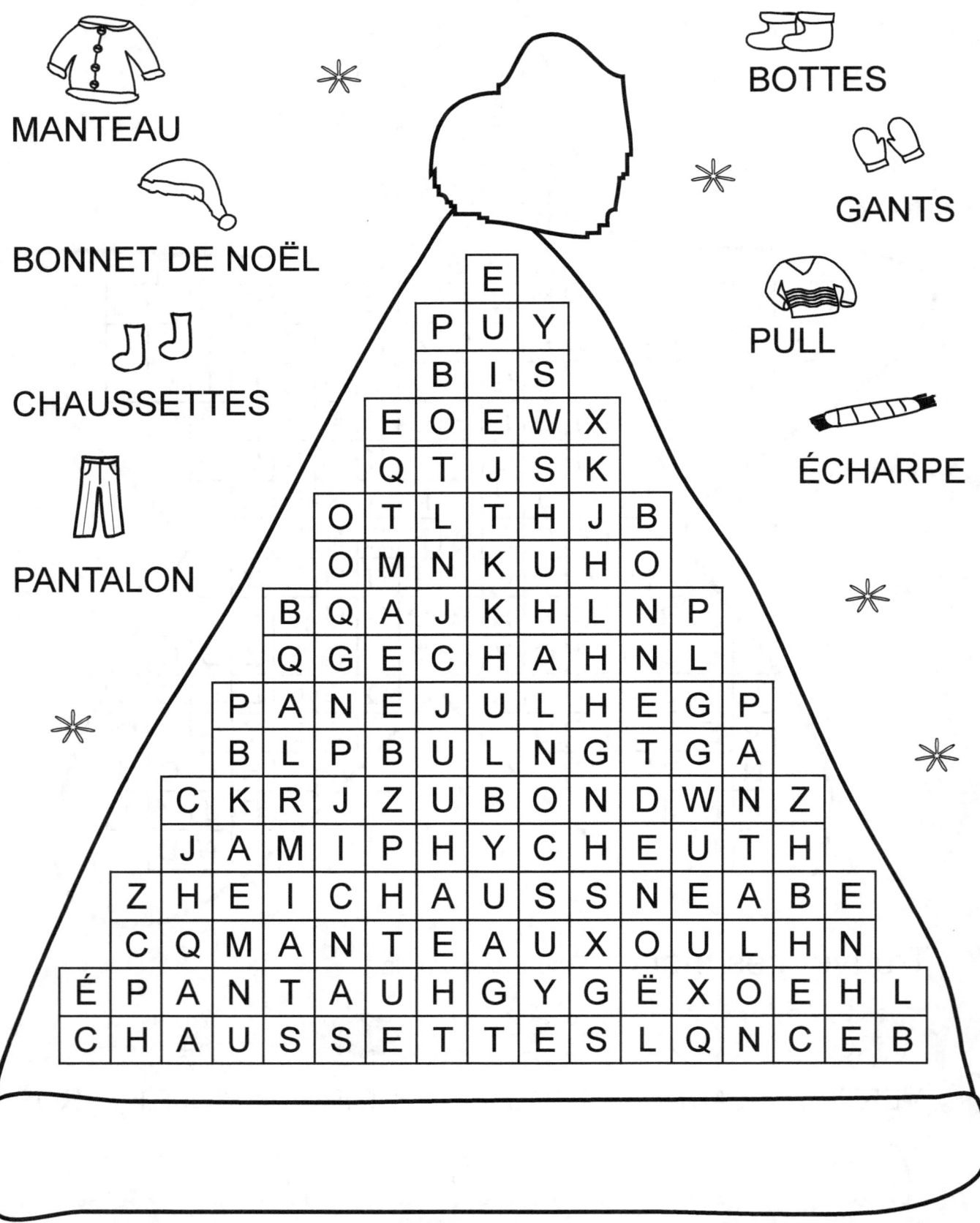

MANTEAU
BONNET DE NOËL
CHAUSSETTES
PANTALON
BOTTES
GANTS
PULL
ÉCHARPE

Les cadeaux (presents)

Trouver ces mots: (Find these words:)

BATEAU   TRAIN   VOITURE   POUPÉE   BALLON

 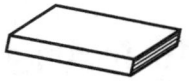 

BONBONS   LIVRE   CRAYONS    NOUNOURS

B	A	T	E	A	U	E	N	B	A	L	I	H	N	H
C	D	E	F	B	S	E	V	B	E	C	L	I	V	L
N	E	C	V	O	I	T	U	R	E	C	A	E	G	Z
C	N	O	U	N	O	H	G	B	X	R	E	G	N	I
B	O	N	H	Y	G	B	E	G	T	F	G	O	B	K
K	I	N	B	H	G	R	F	H	J	Y	L	J	K	Y
X	J	K	H	K	V	L	K	I	H	L	G	B	G	W
T	H	M	N	I	H	B	V	G	A	Y	H	G	V	M
X	Y	H	L	C	R	A	Y	B	J	K	I	J	B	E
X	C	E	G	C	G	T	B	A	T	E	U	J	K	C
C	R	E	H	V	O	I	T	H	Y	G	J	K	L	U
V	A	E	B	E	K	P	O	U	P	É	E	V	O	H
X	Y	D	E	G	E	G	N	O	U	H	Y	G	L	K
C	O	E	B	B	O	N	B	O	N	S	C	E	G	Z
T	N	X	D	G	E	G	L	I	V	W	G	G	E	S
K	S	L	J	H	B	N	O	U	N	O	U	R	S	O

Lets play some games!

To play the Christmas games on the following pages, you can either photocopy the games, play the games directly in the book, or with an adult carefully cut the games out of the book.

If you are playing the games directly in the book it may be useful to put something like a book or a pencil case on the top of the book to hold the page down.

Things you will need:

For counters you can use things like rubbers, cubes or counters from other games you have. Just check the counters you use aren't too big for the games.   If you have a piece of paper or card, you could even make your own counters!

Some games require a dice, but if you don't have one you could cut a piece of paper into small pieces, and write the numbers from one to six on them. Then, instead of rolling a dice you could randomly pick a card with numbers 1 to 6 on.

Remember to say the French words whilst you play the games!

Start at "départ", roll the dice and count that number of spaces. Say the word you land on in French. Take turns to roll the dice. To win, arrive first at "arrivée!"

 une étoile    un ange    Père Noël    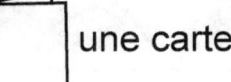 une carte

Start at "départ", roll the dice and count that number of spaces. If the final square you land on has the bottom of the ladder in it go up it, or if it has the head of a snake go down it. Say the word for the space you land on in French. Take turns to roll the dice. To win, arrive first at "arrivée."

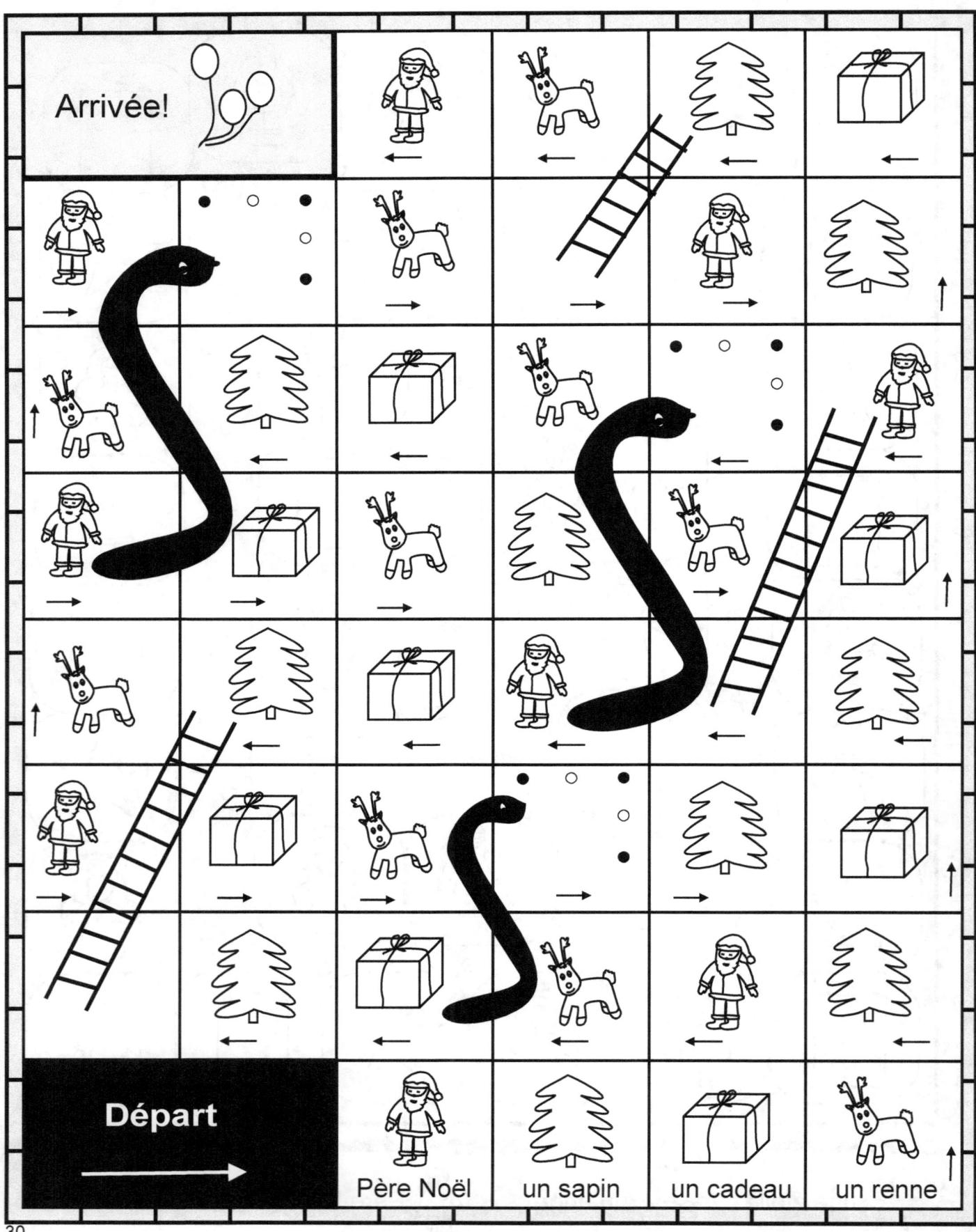

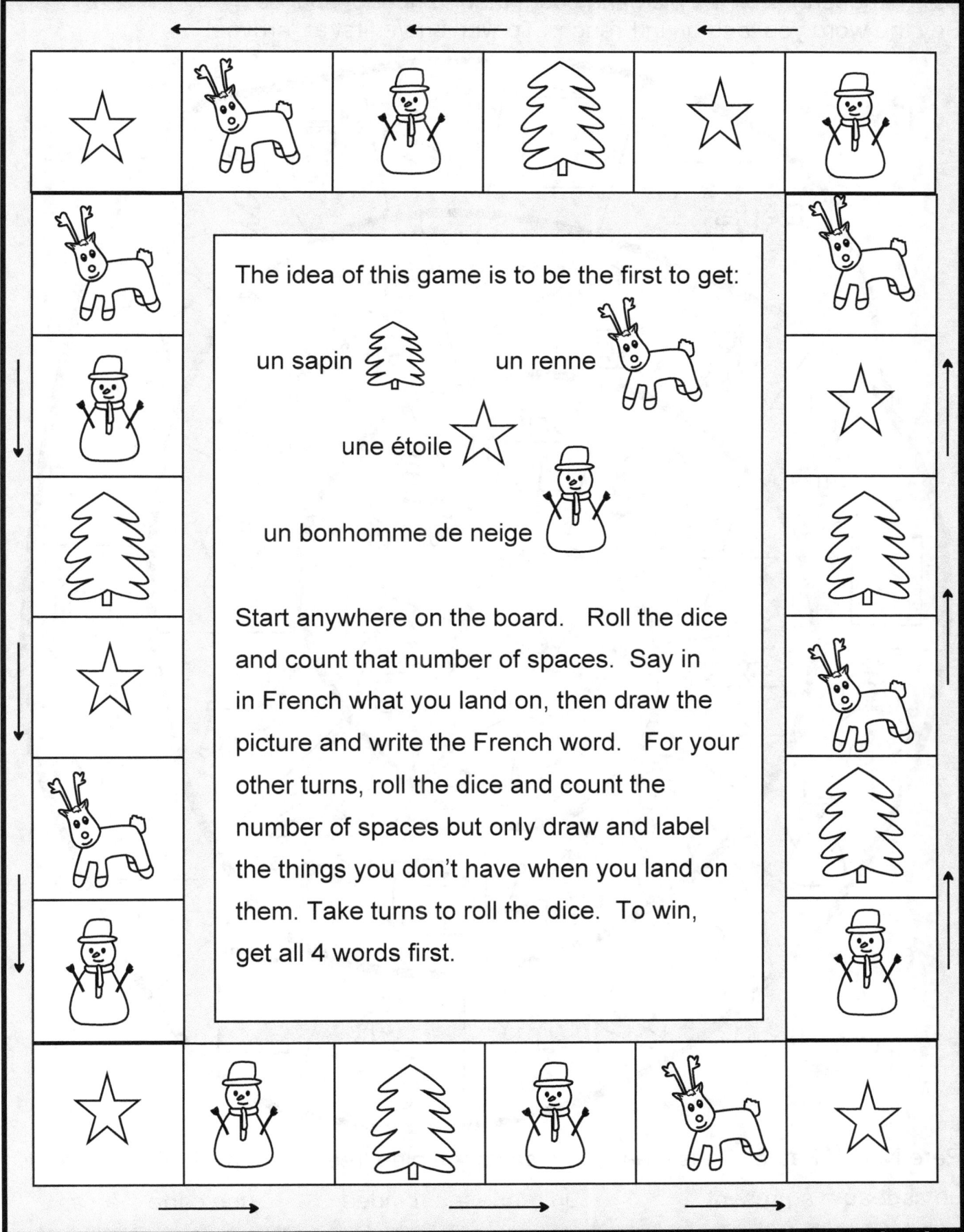

Start at "départ", roll the dice and count that number of spaces.
Say the word you land on in French. To win, arrive first at "arrivée!"

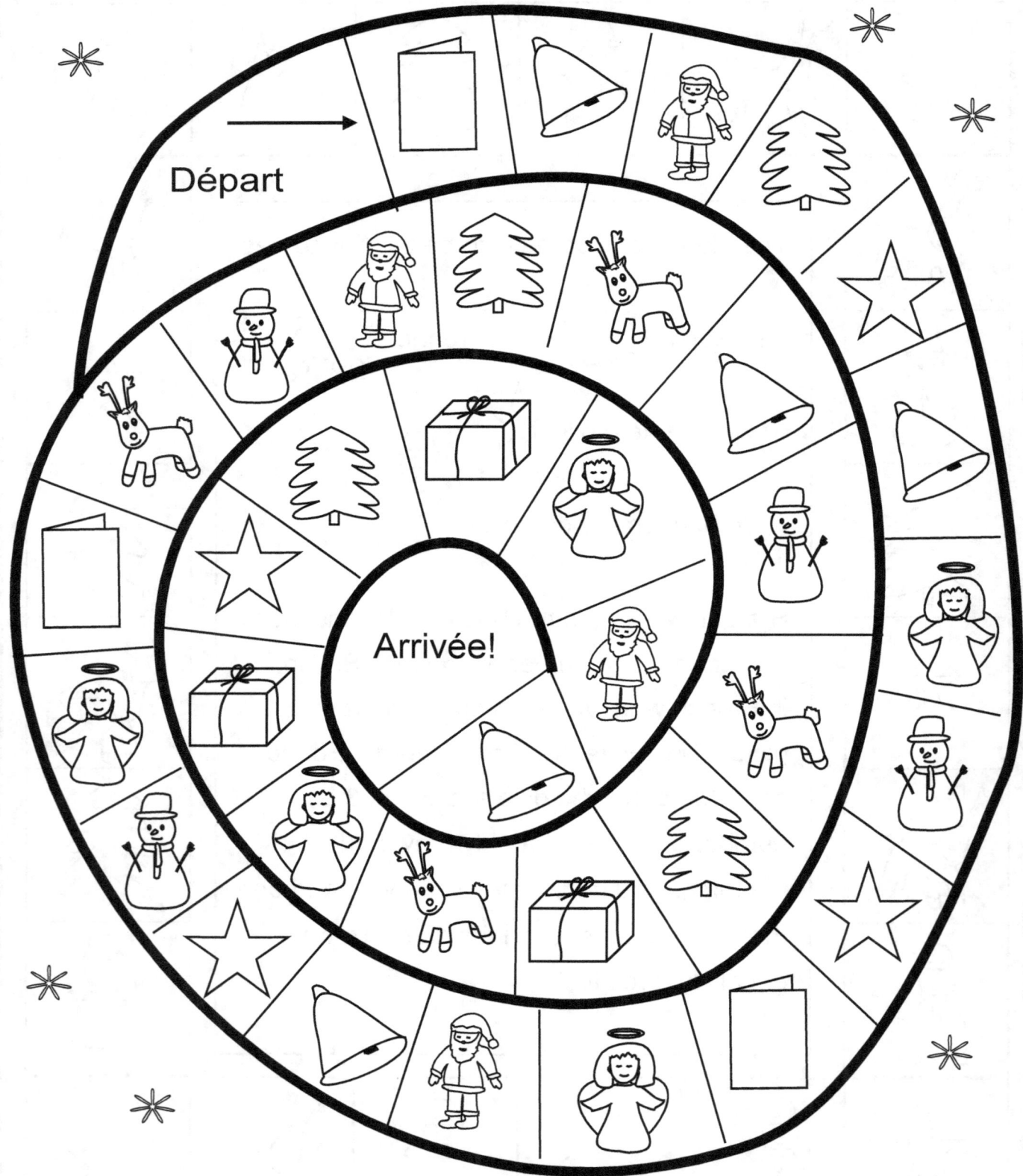

Père Noël = Father Christmas   un sapin = a pine tree   une étoile = a star
un cadeau = a present   un renne = a reindeer   une carte = a card
un bonhomme de neige = snowman   un ange = an angel   une cloche = a bell

Each person / team needs 5 coloured counters or cubes of one colour (or a set of noughts or a set of crosses). Say the French word for the picture shown as you place your counter. Take turns to choose a picture. To win you have to get 3 in a row (vertically, horizontally or diagonally).

Père Noël = Father Christmas   un sapin = a pine tree   une étoile = a star

un cadeau = a present   un renne = a reindeer   une carte = a card

un bonhomme de neige = snowman   un ange = an angel   une cloche = a bell

Lets make french Christmas cards !

There are two sizes of Christmas cards in this book:

The small size is designed to be folded in 4, so even when on paper the Christmas cards should stand up. The Christmas greeting may look like it's upside down, but when you fold the card in 4, the greeting is inside the card and the correct way up!

The larger cards fold in 2. You can write your own greeting in the card. Here are some useful phrases:

Joyeux Noël ………….. Happy Christmas

et………..…..………. and

Bonne année …………. Happy New year

If you want, you can photocopy the Christmas cards to make numerous cards. To avoid photocopying and getting black lines from the photocopier on the cards, photocopy first one copy on white paper, then check if you have any black lines from the photocopier. If you do, cover the black lines with white paper before photocopying the quantity of cards you want. To be sure the Christmas card will fold correctly use a ruler to check where half way from the top would be. The front of the card should be below where half way is. If for some reason your photocopy hasn't turned out that way, rearrange the original on the photocopier, and do another photocopy.

If you don't have a photocopier, ask an adult if they can cut the Christmas cards out of the book for you. All the Christmas cards that appear in this book are followed by a blank page in case you want to use them as cards.

The smaller card folds in 4

The larger card folds in 2

Joyeux Noël
et
Bonne année

Joyeux Noël

Joyeux Noël
et
Bonne année

French - English word list

French		English		French		English	
un	ange	an	angel		jaune		yellow
	anglais		English		Je m'appelle…		My name is …
	Au revoir		Good bye		Joyeux Noël		Happy Christmas
un	ballon	a	ball	un	livre	a	book
un	bateau	a	boat	un	manteau	a	coat
	blanc		white		marron		brown
	bleu		blue		merci		thank you
des	bonbons	some	sweets		neuf		nine
	Bonjour		Good day		Noël		Christmas
	Bonne année		Happy new year		noir		black
un	bonnet de Noël	a	Christmas hat		non		no
des	bottes	some	boots		orange		orange
	Ça va bien		I'm good		oui		yes
	Ça va mal		I'm not good	un	pantalon		trousers
un	cadeau	a	present		Père Noël		Father Christmas
une	carte	a	card	une	poupée	a	doll
un	chat	a	cat	un	pull	a	jumper
des	chaussettes	some	socks		quatre		four
un	chien	a	dog	un	renne	a	reindeer
	cinq		five		rose		pink
une	cloche	a	bell		rouge		red
	Comme ci comme ça		I'm okay		Salut		Hi / Bye
	Comment ça va?		How are you?	un	sapin	a	pine tree
	Comment t'appelles-tu?		What is your name?		sept		seven
des	crayons	some	pencils		s'il vous plaît		please
des	décorations	some	decorations		six		six
	deux		two	un	train	a	train
	dix		ten		trois		three
une	écharpe	a	scarf		un		one
	français		French		vert		green
des	gants	some	gloves		violet		lilac
	gris		grey	une	voiture	a	car
	huit		eight				

Answers

Page 4
On the jumper there should be: 3 trees, 5 stars, 2 snowmen, 8 presents

Page 5
deux sapins   quatre cadeaux   cinq cartes   trois rennes   trois bonhommes de neige

Page 6
dix cadeaux = 10 presents   six cadeaux = 6 presents
trois cadeaux = 3 presents   cinq cadeaux = 5 presents   deux cadeaux = 2 presents
neuf cadeaux = 9 presents   sept cadeaux = 7 presents

Page 8
The presents should be: 5 in yellow   2 in blue   3 in red   4 in pink   6 in green

Pages 9 - 13
1 = yellow   2 = lilac   3 = green   4 = pink   5 = grey   6 = red   7 = brown   8 = black
9 = orange   10 = blue   11 = white

Page 15
1) une voiture   2) une poupée   3) un bateau   4) un train   5) un ballon   6) un nounours

Page 16
1) un nounours   2) un ballon   3) un train   4) une voiture   5) un bateau   6) une poupée

Page 17
a) a car   b) some pencils   c) sweets   d) teddy

Page 20
1) un bonnet de Noël   2) un pull   3) un pantalon   4) un manteau   5) une écharpe
6) des gants   7) des bottes   8) des chaussettes

Page 21
1a) un bonnet rouge et blanc   b) un manteau rouge et blanc   c) des gants marron
d) un pantalon rouge   e) des bottes noires

2a) faux (false)   b) vrai (true)   c) faux (false)   d) vrai (true)

Page 22
un manteau
un pull
des gants
des chaussettes
une écharpe
un bonnet de Noël

Page 23
The jumpers should be coloured as follows:
2 in red, 3 in brown, 4 in green,
3 in grey, 4 in blue.

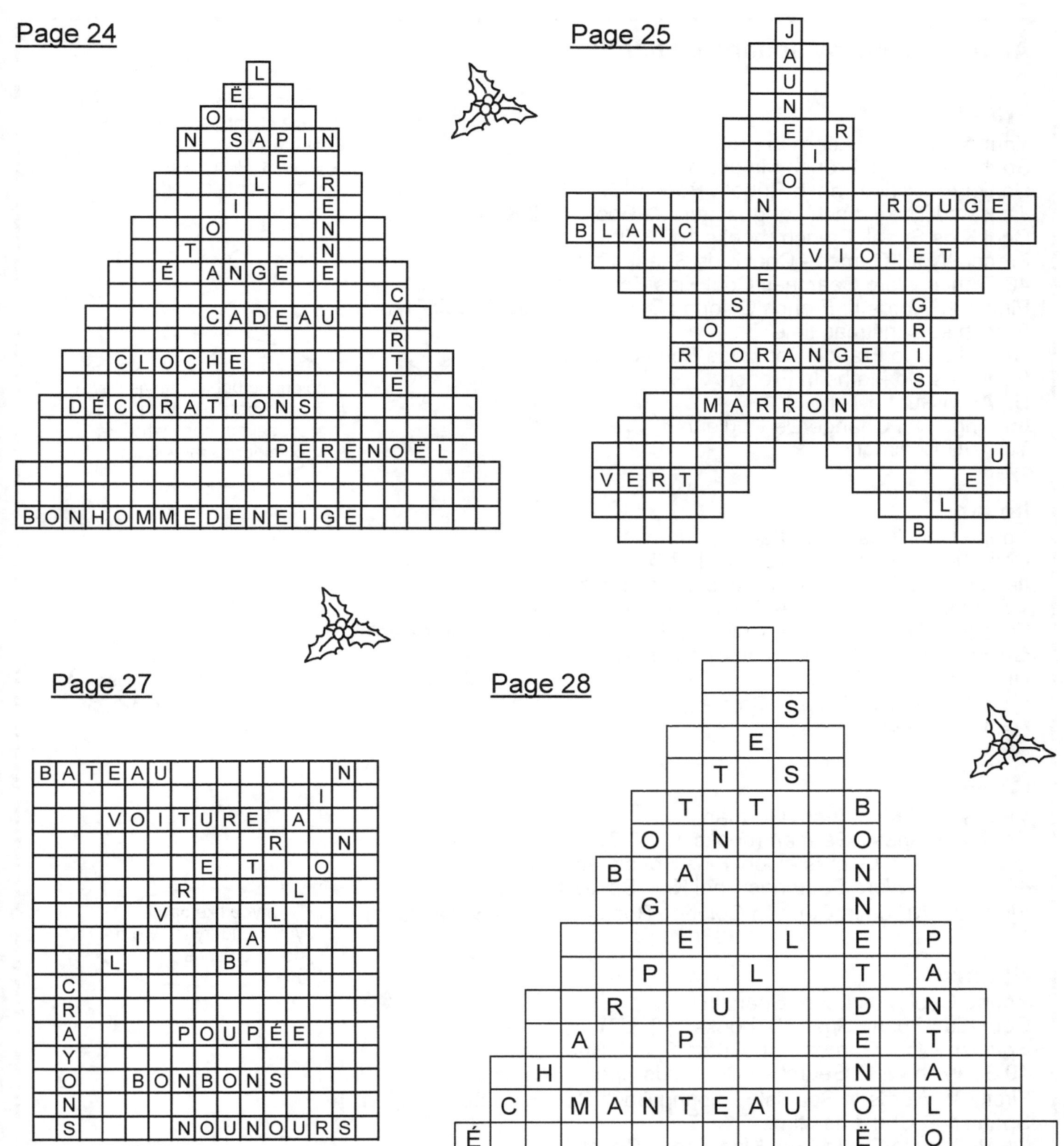

Also available by Joanne Leyland:

French
Young Cool Kids Learn French
Sophie And The French Magician
Daniel And The French Robot - Books 1, 2 & 3
Jack And The French Languasaurus - Books 1, 2 & 3
Cool Kids Speak French (books 1, 2 & 3)
French Word Games - Cool Kids Speak French
40 French Word Searches Cool Kids Speak French
First 100 Words In French Coloring Book Cool Kids Speak French
French at Christmas time
On Holiday In France Cool Kids Speak French
Cool Kids Do Maths In French
Un Alien Sur La Terre
Le Singe Qui Change De Couleur
Tu As Un Animal?

Italian
Young Cool Kids Learn Italian
Cool Kids Speak Italian (books 1, 2 & 3)
Italian Word Games - Cool Kids Speak Italian
40 Italian Word Searches Cool Kids Speak Italian
First 100 Words In Italian Coloring Book Cool Kids Speak Italian
On Holiday In Italy Cool Kids Speak Italian
Un Alieno Sulla Terra
La Scimmia Che Cambia Colore
Hai Un Animale Domestico?

German
Young Cool Kids Learn German
Cool Kids Speak German (books 1, 2 & 3)
German Word Games - Cool Kids Speak German
40 German Word Searches Cool Kids Speak German
First 100 Words In German Coloring Book Cool Kids Speak German

Spanish
Young Cool Kids Learn Spanish
Cool Kids Speak Spanish (books 1, 2 & 3)
Spanish Word Games - Cool Kids Speak Spanish
40 Spanish Word Searches Cool Kids Speak Spanish
First 100 Words In Spanish Coloring Book Cool Kids Speak Spanish
Spanish at Christmas time
On Holiday In Spain Cool Kids Speak Spanish
Cool Kids Do Maths In Spanish
Un Extraterrestre En La Tierra
El Mono Que Cambia De Color
Seis Mascotas Maravillosas

The word search editions have 40 topics in each book. The word searches are in fun shapes. Pictures accompany the words to find.

The first 100 words colouring book editions have 3 or 4 words per page, and are ideal for those who like to colour as they learn.

The stories in a foreign language have an English translation at the back.

If you like games, you could try the word game editions.

The holiday editions have essential words & phrases in part 1. And in part 2 there are challenges to use these words whilst away.

For more information on the books available, and different ways of learning a foreign language go to https://learnforeignwords.com